Sounds Intriguing

Sounds Intriguing

Alan Maley
Alan Duff

Cambridge University Press
Cambridge
London · New York · Melbourne

Published by the Syndics of the Cambridge University Press
The Pitt Building, Trumpington Street, Cambridge CB2 1RP
Bentley House, 200 Euston Road, London NW1 2DB
32 East 57th Street, New York, NY 10022, USA
296 Beaconsfield Parade, Middle Park, Melbourne 3206,
Australia

© Cambridge University Press 1979

First published 1979

Phototypeset in V.I.P. Bembo by
Western Printing Services Ltd, Bristol
Printed in Great Britain at the
University Press, Cambridge

ISBN 0 521 22138 2 Book
ISBN 0 521 22135 8 Cassette

Contents

Acknowledgements

Thanks are due to the following for permission to reproduce poems: p. 69, Ward Lock Educational Ltd; pp. 69–70, J. M. Dent & Sons Ltd; pp. 70–1, Atheneum Publishers Inc. Thanks are also due to Lorrimer Publishing Ltd for permission to reproduce the extract from a film script on p. 71.

Introduction

What are sound sequences?

They are, simply, sequences of sound that suggest a story. The story is not inherent in the sounds themselves but in the listener's interpretation of them.

The sequences are short (few are longer than one minute) and self-contained. Some provide the framework for a complete incident, some concentrate on only one part of the incident, and some give no more than a few powerful suggestions, e.g. sound of voices, chattering dies down, loud gong. So, the kind of story that can be built around each will be very different – there will be mystery tales, surprises, accidents, dreams, jokes, etc.

Why use sound sequences?

In life, two people who witness the same incident may end up giving very different accounts of what they saw. This is one of the reasons why many court cases drag on for months! It is natural for people to interpret, to colour what they see or hear with their own moods and attitudes. This need to give one's *own* account is often thwarted in highly controlled language teaching situations.

With the sound sequences, the listener is stimulated to *want* or *need* to say what he thinks, without fear of correction. Because there are no absolutely 'correct' interpretations each person has the right to express his own opinion and defend it in open discussion. And because no two people think alike, everyone's interest is fully engaged. The problem of 'what to talk about' disappears.

When working from a text, one is bound by words. What is written is written; discussion centres on the printed page. Working with sounds, however, one is no longer bound. The sounds are only *part* of a context, which would normally be *seen* as well. So, although everyone hears the 'same' sounds, they are free from the start to build their own mental picture of what is happening. Even at the level of recognition – let alone

1

interpretation – there will be differences between individuals. It is these differences that spark off discussion.

There are, of course, many other ways of stimulating people to talk: pictures, logical problems, simulations, dramatisation and imaginative listening, are just some of the many ways of arousing the *desire* to speak. (For further creative ideas see the works listed in the Bibliography.) Nevertheless, we should not forget that we are exposed to sound throughout nearly all our waking lives. It would be a pity indeed to neglect this powerful stimulus.

Level

Everyone works to his own level, since each student's responses are adjusted naturally to whatever happens to be the level of the group. With texts, one may justifiably speak of 'difficult' or 'easy' language because the level is set by the words and structures, but with sounds there is no implicit level. Sounds in themselves are neither 'difficult' nor 'easy'. The better students will, of course, be able to offer more complex interpretations but not necessarily more interesting ones. Students with even a restricted command of the language are still able to take an active part in the discussion because their interpretations are not bound by structures.

One final – and important – advantage of this material is its *flexibility*. The sequences are extremely short, and the amount of time spent on them depends entirely on the needs of the class. The same sequence may be used on one occasion for only a few minutes – to fill in a gap or rouse a drowsy class – and on another occasion be extended over a whole lesson or even longer.

How to use the sequences

The following general points need to be made:

a) the sequences have not been 'graded' or arranged in any special order. There is therefore no need to work through them from 1–21 unless you feel so inclined;

b) how frequently or how intensively you use them is also a matter for personal judgement;

c) given that the sequences do not constitute a language course in themselves but may be used to supplement a course, it will obviously be useful to see how certain sequences fit into the overall course scheme. In many cases it will be found that the

2

themes, vocabulary, structures or functions associated with a given sequence fit particularly well with, for example, a course-book unit. This may help you decide when to use which sequence.

In working with the sound sequences, the students are not solving a problem to which there is only one 'correct' answer; they are, rather, offering creative interpretations of what they hear. And there is absolutely no reason why several interpretations should not be equally valid. This means that whatever questions may be asked are intended not to produce 'correct' answers but to stimulate reflection. Although these questions may be put to the class as a whole, they should preferably be considered by the individual, alone or in small groups. The aim of the exercise is to produce several different interpretations, which will later be defended (or attacked) by referring back to the same sequence of sounds. One is looking for diversity, not unanimity. A comparison might be made with the famous Rorschach 'ink blot' test, in which people are shown abstract designs and asked to describe what they 'see'; all interpretations are interesting precisely because they are different, and yet based on the same stimulus.

Suggested procedure for playing the sequences

Irrespective of the detailed oral work laid down for each sequence, it will be necessary to play the sequence through *at least three times*. During the first playing, the students should be asked simply to listen 'with their minds open'. During the second playing, they should be asked to jot down *what* they hear (i.e. the actual sounds, not an immediate interpretation of them, for example, 'the crash of breaking glass' not 'someone dropping a vase'). You may or may not wish to have a class discussion at this point. During the third (and any subsequent playing), the students should make notes on their interpretation of what they have heard. The writing should be done before group discussion begins. This is to avoid, as far as possible, domination of the discussion by more forthcoming students. If everyone has something down on paper, they are less tempted to adopt the ideas put forward by the others. The guideline questions can easily be written on the board or the overhead projector. All oral production and writing exercises have been so worded that the teachers may read the questions or instructions directly to the students.

3

Format for each sequence

The teaching material for each sequence is divided into six sections:

Soundscript

This gives the basic outline of what is to be heard on the tape. We have kept this description as general as possible so as to prevent users of the material from jumping to one particular interpretation before they have thought about others, 'taxi pulling up at the kerb' gives specific details which preclude other interpretations, whereas 'noise of engine' leaves the interpretation much more open.

Possible lines of questioning

This is to guide the student's attention to the key features in interpreting the sequence. The questions are by no means exhaustive, nor need they all be answered. In fact, after a short time, the students become accustomed to these questions without prompting, since the basic questions must always be asked.

Where is this taking place? (Is it all happening in the same place?)
How many people are there?
Who are they?
Is there any connection between X and Y?
What is it?
When is this taking place? (Time of day).
What is the *weather* like? (Is this significant?)
Why does X *happen*?
What happens next?

Most sequences do however require additional specific guideline questions.

Suggestions for oral work

Here we have tried to suggest interesting ways of using the language to work out solutions to the problem the sequence sets. In most cases we advocate work in pairs or groups, and it is important that – at least to begin with – the instructions are scrupulously observed. If it says 'work in groups of four', the students should work in fours, not threes or sixes.

4

The principle of asking students to move from one group to another is also important, since it leads to real interaction and interchange. Try to encourage students to speculate about more than one interpretation before deciding on their version.

Suggestions for writing

Here again, it is important that students do precisely what they are asked and not something else.

The writing tasks we have set are rarely meant to be done by the individual on his own, since we believe writing to be the most difficult skill to acquire and the one in which students profit most from pooling their knowledge and abilities.

Whenever we ask for the writing to be done in a particular style, e.g. newspaper headlines, telegrams, verse, etc. we suggest that authentic models be provided for the students to base their work on (see Appendix 2 for suggestions).

Vocabulary

The more important sounds and the words associated with them have been dealt with in this section. We have tried to be as systematic as possible by giving synonyms, antonyms, and hyponyms, by making reference to basic semantic parameters of sounds (such as length, pitch, loudness, etc.) and by giving their common collocations (i.e. the words with which they are commonly associated). In Appendix 1 the vocabulary of sounds in English is grouped by reference to the way the sounds are produced (see page 60).

It is worthwhile here, however, to set out some of the basic criteria according to which sounds can be grouped:

short / long (e.g. sniff, wail)
high pitch / low pitch (e.g. fizz, bubble)
loud / soft (e.g. pound, tap)
heavy / light (e.g. thump, jingle)
resonant / dull (e.g. clang, thud)
single / repeated or continuous (e.g. bang, patter, trickle)
regular / irregular (e.g. gush, spurt)
rapid / slow (e.g. whirr, chug)
intense / relaxed (e.g. squirt, lap)
concordant / discordant (e.g. chime, jangle)
caused by an agent / made by self (e.g. rumble, snip)

5

human agent / animal agent / mechanical agent (e.g. whisper, bark, tick)

material: wood, metal, water, paper, cloth, etc. (e.g. creak, scrape, gurgle, rustle)

sounds that are also movements (e.g. slam, thump)

All these can of course, vary in intensity, i.e. they may become louder or softer.

One way of developing a systematic control of sound vocabulary is by grouping words by reference to these parameters. Any two words may be associated with several parameters (the examples in brackets illustrate only their association to the parameter given). For example, *fizz* is high-pitched, light, continuous, rapid, intense made by itself, liquid; *boom* is long, low-pitched, usually loud, heavy, resonant, continuous, slow, concordant, often connected with metal or waves.

It is *not* suggested that students be made to learn the characteristics inherent in each word (that is, before collocation, associative meaning etc. are added). But it is certainly useful for the teacher to be aware of these basic, generalisable qualities, since they may help him to frame questions which throw into relief for the learner the essential quality of a given word.

The kinds of questions we have in mind are, for example:

– which of the following things would *clatter* if you dropped them?
– which of these words describes a longer / louder / higher sound?
– can wood make a *chinking* sound?
– can we say there was a *sharp thud*?
– is *snap* short or long?
– which kinds of things can *splinter*?

It is recommended that teachers prepare questions of this kind in addition to any which may be given in the book.

Appendix 1 was produced in part to help teachers with this preparation. It will also be useful to make fairly frequent reference to it before checking a word in a dictionary.

Possible interpretations

The interpretations we have given are emphatically *only* possibilities. In no circumstances should they be thought of as 'better' solutions than the ones the students suggest. Indeed, they should not be referred to at all unless no one has any idea of what might be going on, or unless the class insists on knowing what the sequence 'really' was. In the latter case, one of the interpretations can be presented as the 'real' one.

Language functions needed

The basic activity for the students in all the sequences, both in the preparation for the writing and for the further oral work, is *discussion*, involving *coming to agreement* about the subject under discussion. If this type of language interaction is analysed it can be shown to comprise a number of essential language functions (e.g. asking for someone else's opinion). A list of these essential functions, together with examples, is set out below. These functions fall into two basic types: language used to organise the way the discussion takes place (transactional language) and language used to talk about the subject under discussion (discussion language).

a) *Transactional language*
   Getting started e.g. Right. What about the first noise?
                         O.K.
                         Come on then.
   Making suggestions/proposals e.g. Let's listen to it again first.
   (for a course of action)
   Giving directives e.g. You take the notes Peter.
   Negotiating agreement e.g. Does everyone agree?
                                 Is that O.K. then?
   Summarising e.g. So, first of all, he is . . .
                     Right, let's see if we've got it right.
                     First of all . . .
   Commenting e.g. Not very easy, is it?
                     We'd better hurry.
                     I wish he'd play it again.

b) *Discussion language*
   Stating opinion (on a scale of certainty–uncertainty)
                   e.g. It's a train.
                   It could be an aeroplane I suppose.
   Agreement e.g. That's right.
   (often followed by *Expansion* e.g. A jet)
   Disagreement e.g. I doubt it/I don't think so.
   (often followed by *Counter opinion* e.g. More like a tractor)
   Asking for Information e.g. Was it before or after the crash?

Asking for someone's opinion e.g. What about you Dick?
What do you think?
Asking for confirmation e.g. It was a shot, wasn't it?
Asking for clarification e.g. A what? What sort of machine?

Sequence 1

Soundscript

Water (lapping) – humming – water (gushing) – pause –
humming – silence – water lapping – sudden shout.

Possible lines of questioning

- How many people are involved in this incident? What are they
  doing? Is it enjoyable or not?
- Is this taking place indoors or outdoors? If indoors, what sort
  of room is it? If outdoors, where is it? By the sea? In a park?
  etc.
- How long has the activity been going on?
- What is the reason for the sudden shout at the end? What has
  he 'got'?
- Does this remind you of any incident you have witnessed or
  read about?

Suggestions for oral work

In groups of three or four decide on an interpretation for this
sequence. Then decide how the action will continue. (What
happens next? Do other people come in? etc.)

When this has been done, groups work out a brief mime
sequence to illustrate the whole scene. The groups observe each
others' mimes, then take them over and add words (e.g. Group 1
observes Group 2, and vice versa. Then Group 2 re-does Group
1's scene, but adding words of their own.)

One person from each group moves to the next group and
presents to it the version of the story his previous group has
worked out. The group should try to find as many objections as
possible to this story before giving their version.

Suggestions for writing

- Each group should write a poem of *six lines* about the incident.
  Remember that a poem does not have to rhyme.

9

– In groups, write a headline for a newspaper article about this incident. Before starting, look at some real English newspaper headlines.

Vocabulary

– Which of the following would *not* produce a *humming* sound?
a wire along which electricity is passing
a bee trapped in a bottle
an aeroplane heard from a long way away
a man singing a tune with his lips closed
a motor-car engine when the car is waiting (not moving)

– Which of these words would indicate *fear* on the part of the person who made the noise described?

shout	scream
howl	shriek
roar	squeal

– Do any of the above indicate *pain* caused to the person making the noise? or *anger*?
One of these words does not have overtones of fear, pain, or anger. Which is it?

– All the following sounds are associated with water (or liquids)
splash
lap
drip
dribble
gush
gurgle
bubble

Splash is a violent movement, usually caused by something or someone falling into or agitating the water, whereas *lap* is a gentle movement made by the water itself.
Drip is a repeated sound, usually slow.
Dribble indicates a small quantity of water moving (falling), whereas *gush* is a violent powerful movement (usually following a release of pressure).
Gurgle is the noise made when water drains away down a smallish hole.
Bubble is the noise made when water or some other fluid is boiling or is violently disturbed.

Which of the above words would be used to describe the noise made by the water or fluid in these situations?
- a tap which cannot be turned off completely
- a kettle boiling
- a lorry going through a puddle of water
- water against the shore of a lake when a slight breeze is blowing
- water running out of the bath when the plug has been pulled out
- water as it comes out of a hydro-electric barrage
- water in the bed of a stream after a month without rain

- These sounds (splash etc.) are partly distinguished by the length of time they last (long, short, or intermittent), partly by their volume (loud or soft) and partly by their pitch (high or low), e.g.

splash – short / loud / high
bubble – long / soft or medium low
gurgle – long / soft / low
gush   – long / loud / high
drip   – intermittent / soft / high
lap   – intermittent / soft / low

These features of length, volume and pitch also serve to distinguish other sound words and they will come up again later in the book.

Possible interpretations

- A man in his bath doing a crossword puzzle; he suddenly finds the answer to a difficult clue.
- Archimedes lying in his bath notices something interesting about the water level. He has discovered Archimedes' law!
- A man in a research laboratory is trying to find the right amount of what to put in a solution which will make people invisible. After a long series of experiments, he finally discovers the formula. (Some of the solution has accidentally spilt on his hand, which has disappeared!)
- A spy is developing a film in the bathroom, and is overjoyed to find that the photograph of a missile base has come out.
- An explorer has just returned from a long expedition to the Tropics. This is the first bath he has had in a long time. Suddenly he notices an awful change in his skin condition, and realises he has caught an incurable disease.

Sequence 2

Soundscript

Hubbub of voices – clinking – subdued conversation – loud
ripping / tearing – coughing – silence.

Possible lines of questioning

– Does this sequence take place inside or outside? If inside,
  where? (A large hall, small empty room, private home?) If
  outside, where? (On land, on the sea, in a city?) What time of
  day is it? What is the weather like?
– How many people are involved? More than two? More than
  ten? More than fifty? Are they standing? Sitting? Travelling?
– How are they dressed? How long have they been here? How
  long are they going to stay?
– Towards the end of the sequence a cough is heard? How many
  people cough – all, some, very few, one only?
– Does any person or any thing enter during the sequence?
– Is whatever happens in the sequence expected or unexpected?

Suggestions for oral work

In groups of three, discuss your answers to the questions
above. Then decide (a) what causes the sudden silence, (b)
how long the silence will last, (c) what will happen in the next
sixty seconds.

One person from each group should now move to another
group. The newcomer should find out from the new group
what their interpretation is. He should also explain his. Now,
one person from each group is to be a journalist. He is to go
round to as many groups as he can finding out what happened
in the sequence. Group members must imagine they were
present at this event. They should tell the journalist *their*
version of the story. He may interrupt, question, ask for
clarification, etc. He should take *notes*.

Suggestions for writing

- The journalists must produce a story to fit a quarter column, i.e. about 150 words – not more. The eye-witnesses will read these stories aloud in their groups. They may then call on the journalist to justify what he wrote.
- Alternatively, imagine that you were directly affected by what happened in the sequence. Write a note of *apology*, *complaint*, or *thanks* (depending on your interpretation) to the person responsible for what happened. In the following class, hand your note to someone else. You must now *reply* to the note you have received.

  (Remember: it is advisable to listen to the sequence once again before the written exercise is done.)

Vocabulary

- Which of the following would not produce a *clinking* sound:
  a glass against another glass
  a wooden chair being pulled across a wooden floor
  an iron chain against another chain
  a rock against a rock
  a knife and fork on a plate
  Which of the above would produce a *scraping* sound?

- Which of the following is the *least serious* form of conversation:
  discussing
  chatting
  debating
  conferring

- Consider the following words: *cut, tear, hack, slash, rip*. *Hack, slash* and *rip* are rapid, violent movements; *tear* and *cut* are slower, more deliberate. With *hack* and *slash*, some instrument (e.g. a knife, axe, chopper) would nearly always be used; with *cut*, the instrument might be smaller (e.g. a razor-blade, scissors); with *tear* and *rip*, the hands could be used, or some object might be involved (e.g. barbed-wire, a nail). Here are some situations in which these words might occur:
  - making your way through thick jungle (*hack, cut*)
  - making bandages from a shirt (*tear, rip*)
  - a fireman breaking through a window covered by heavy curtains (*slash*)
  - a shopkeeper measuring cloth (*cut*)

    − a convict making an escape-rope from sheets (*rip*, *tear*)
    In each case decide what the person *uses* to perform the action.

− We do not always *cough* because we have a cold. We also
   cough when we are:
   embarrassed
   want to attract someone's attention
   want to fill a silence
   want to express disapproval

− When silence falls, it may happen for many different reasons.
   Consider the difference between:
   fall silent
   keep quiet
   shut up
   stop talking

Possible interpretations

− An agricultural / farming show. Farmer J. has just won first
   prize for his black Friesland bull. He goes into the restaurant
   tent to celebrate, leaving the bull in the charge of his young
   son. The bull wants to celebrate as well, so he starts testing his
   horns on the tent canvas . . .
− An official banquet for the National Union of Journalists. The
   after-dinner speaker (who disapproves of banquets and 'that
   sort of thing') is wearing a dinner jacket borrowed for the
   occasion. As he raises his arm for silence the jacket splits down
   the side.
− Summer. Dinner on the deck of a luxury yacht. Guests are
   eating on deck. One man (brother-in-law of the yacht owner)
   is talking excitedly, waving his arms about. His fork catches in
   the sail – a new silk sail worth three thousand pounds . . .
− Small private dinner party. The hostess is wearing a long
   white dress. The guest on her right has accidently moved his /
   her chair so that the leg is resting on the white dress. When the
   hostess stands up to go to the kitchen . . .

Sequence 3

Soundscript

Mechanical humming – rustling – clinking – trundling sound – sudden whistling / rushing + increase in noise – shout (three times) – metallic noise – noise of engines receding – thin noise – silence – crowd noise.

Possible lines of questioning

- Does all the action happen in the same place? If not, how many places are involved and where are they? (In a city? The countryside? In a house? A factory? A field? . . .)
- How many people are involved in the sequence? What is their relationship with each other? (Do they know each other well? Is one of them more important than the others? etc.)
- Why is there a sudden increase of noise at one point? And why does it die away again?
- Can you tell what time of day it is? Day or night? Morning or evening?
- How do you explain the last sounds in the sequence? How are they connected to the earlier part of the story?

Suggestions for oral work

Work in groups of three or four and try to find the answers to the above questions. They will help you to find an interpretation.

When every group has found a story, one person from each group should go to another group. This group should try to find out what his story is by asking him questions to which the answer is *yes* or *no* (*not quite*, *almost*, etc.).

In pairs, draw a cartoon sequence of up to four frames to illustrate the story you have agreed upon.

Suggestions for writing

- Add captions to the cartoons drawn in pairs. These can either be in 'speech balloons' or written underneath the cartoons as dialogue and/or narrative.
- Suppose that you were one of the people who observed this incident. Write a letter to a close friend telling him or her about it.
- Imagine you are a reporter on a local newspaper. Write an article of not more than about 150 words. You want to be promoted in your job, so you make it as sensational as possible.
- Imagine you are one of the people from the beginning of the story. You have to write an official report on what happened for one of your superiors. You try to make it look as if everything that happened was quite normal and that there were no problems.

Vocabulary

- Which of these things could produce a *hum*?
  a lift
  aircraft engines
  distant traffic
  rain on a tin roof

- Make a list of things which make a clinking sound (see vocabulary to Sequence 2, page 13). Is the sound light / high or heavy / low?
- Which of the following things does *not* produce a *rustling* sound?
  opening a newspaper
  walking through dry dead leaves
  brushing shoes
  drawing a curtain
  turning over in bed

- When we *trundle* something, is it a heavy or a light object? Is it on wheels or rollers? Does it make a heavy / regular noise?

- Which sound is louder: *scraping* or *scratching*? Is *scraping* a pleasant sound to listen to?

Possible interpretations

- A party of commandos is parachuting into enemy territory. A sudden change of wind direction makes them drop into the middle of a garden party being held in their General's garden.
- A group of young parachutists on a training flight near the enemy frontier. A change of wind direction carries them into enemy territory, where they come down into the middle of a village fête.
- An air show. The world's greatest team of parachutist-acrobats carry out their act. Unfortunately, a change of wind carries them down into the crowd.
- It is night and a group of illegal immigrants is being smuggled into the country in the back of a big lorry. They are told to jump out of the lorry while it is moving. They are all knocked unconscious. When they come to their senses it is day time and they find themselves at the entrance to a swimming-pool, surrounded by crowds.

Sequence 4

Soundscript

Pop music (continuous throughout) – clinking, clattering – birds – voices – laughter – humming – swishing / cracking – purring – snapping – 'Mary, Mary' – growl – smashing – gasp – pop music continuing.

Possible lines of questioning

- Where is this taking place? (In a house? Out of doors? In a field? In an office?) What is the weather like?
- Can you tell how many people there are? What are they doing at the beginning of the sequence?
- Which country do you think this takes place in?
- Who is Mary? Is she present? When the man says 'Mary' the second time, what can you tell from the tone of his voice?
- Does anything unexpected occur anywhere in the sequence? What causes it?
- Why does the radio go on playing?

Suggestions for oral work

Work in groups of three. One member of each group acts as secretary and writes down in note form all the possible interpretations the group thinks of. When this has been done, decide on *one* interpretation. Now decide what happens immediately after the incident (in the next three minutes). Try to include some dialogue between the people who might be involved.

Suggestions for writing

- Each group should prepare a telegram which one of the people involved in the incident sent later the next day. (Do not forget that with telegrams you pay for every word, so as many words as possible should be left out without changing the sense.)

When this has been done, groups exchange telegrams. Now try to work out from the telegram what must have happened. Write a letter from the person who has received the telegram to a third person, telling him or her all about the incident.

– In pairs, write a headline to an article in a newspaper on the incident.

Vocabulary

– Birds can make the following sounds: *warbling*, *cheeping*, *chirping*, *twittering*, *piping*, *trilling*. Look these words up in the dictionary. Which one best describes the bird noises in this sequence?

– Which of these adjectives could not be used to describe the hum of the traffic in the distance?

steady	muffled
deafening	shrill

– All the following words describe ways of breaking things:

snap	smash
shatter	split

When something *snaps*, it breaks cleanly and immediately. It is usually something *brittle*, like a bone, a pencil, a piece of chalk, a twig or branch, but it can also be something under high pressure, like a wire or a rope. When something *smashes*, it makes a loud noise. It is usually something made of glass or china (clay), though not always. *Fragile* things are also most likely to *shatter* (windows, bottles, glasses and – figuratively – nerves). When we use *shatter* rather than *smash*, we tend to think of the whole thing disintegrating into sharp pieces.

Things which are prone to *splitting* tend to have definite lines of weakness in them (wood, the seams in clothing). A split takes place along these lines, dividing the object into two pieces.

– Which of these animal sounds would cause *fear*?

a growl	a grunt
a hiss	a squeal
a purr	a roar

Does any of them indicate *pain* or *contentment* felt by the animals which make them?

19

– When we *gasp*, is the air drawn into our mouth or pushed out? And when we *sigh*?
We can *gasp* with *surprise*, with *fear*, with *astonishment*, with *excitement*, with *horror*. We can *sigh* with *relief*, with *resignation*, with *irritation*, with *boredom*, with *satisfaction* or *contentment*.

Possible interpretations

– Steve has taken out his girl-friend Mary for a picnic in the woods not far from London. She has just gone back to the car to fetch her bag. Steve thinks he hears her returning through the trees, but when he turns round to look he sees a leopard. Panic-stricken, he remembers reading in the newspaper about a leopard that has escaped from London Zoo . . .
– A father, a mother and their small daughter Mary have stopped for a picnic near the motorway. Mary has gone for a walk with her mother. Before they go, the father has warned them not to go too far because a lion has escaped from a zoo some distance away. This impresses Mary so much that she decides to run away from her mother and come back to frighten her father by pretending to be the lion.
– A millionaire who has built a house in the middle of the jungle is entertaining friends to tea. He keeps a number of wild animals as pets. The new maid, Mary, is not quite used to the animals yet. When she comes back with a fresh pot of tea, she sees a leopard next to the millionaire. She drops the teapot . . .

Sequence 5

Soundscript

'Left right left right left right le-eft . . .' – sound of feet on solid surface – changing to echoing surface – 'Platoon, Halt!' – thud of boots crashing to halt – silence – sound of tap-dance on echoing surface – male laughter – 'Halt!' – tap-dance goes on for a few more steps, then stops – loud applause.

Possible lines of questioning

- Words can be heard in this sequence. Who is speaking? To whom – how many people, and who are they? Where are they? What is the weather like?
- Where have these people come from? Where are they going? They are heard moving over different surfaces: why do the surfaces change?
- Does anything unexpected occur in the sequence? If so, at what point? At a certain moment, laughter is heard. Who is laughing? What at? Is the laughter a sign of amusement, relief, mockery, shock, nervous tension, pleasure . . .?
- Where does the applause come from? Is it necessarily connected with what has gone before?

Suggestions for oral work

Working in groups of three or four, come to an agreement about what actually occurred in this sequence. You should also decide what is going to happen next. One person in the group should make notes.

Now, one person from each group moves to another group. This group should try to find out what his story is by asking him questions to which the answer is *yes* or *no*.

Suggestions for writing

- What happened was intended as a joke. It misfired. The person

who issued the orders has asked for an explanation in writing of what happened. You have been chosen to work out the explanation. Draw up your rough draft, then compare it with your neighbour's. After five to ten minutes, the class should unite to draw up a composite letter of explanation / apology.
- You happened to see this in a foreign country. Write a *postcard* to a close friend describing what happened. (Postcards should be passed round the group to be read aloud.)

Vocabulary

- We hear the sound of *marching* feet: are they *in step* or *out of step*?
- The feet march on different surfaces: which gives the greater *echo*, the *solid* or the *hollow* surface?
- Who gives orders to a platoon of soldiers: the *general*, the *lieutenant*, the *sergeant-major*, the *sergeant*, the *corporal*?
- The *tap-dance* was popular before and during the Second World War. Why does it seem out of place in the context of this sequence?

Possible interpretations

- A war film is being made. The actors have done the same scene seven times in the blazing sun; each time the director is dissatisfied with the marching. The eighth time, one of the actors breaks into a song–and–dance routine to relieve his frustration. His fellow actors are amused, but the director . . .
- Army training camp. A not-too-intelligent sergeant has recently heard that soldiers marching over a wooden bridge can make the bridge collapse. He is determined to prove this is not true. Each day he marches his platoon over the same wooden bridge (14 km from the camp!). This has been going on for a month and the bridge is still intact. Today, one of the privates loses patience . . .
- A small American town. Independence Day celebrations are coming up. The local Officers Training Corps gallantly offers to train the drum majorettes in marching. Twenty majorettes are put in a platoon of men. The sergeant-major delights in marching them through the village square onto the platform (from which speeches will be given) and bringing them to a resounding halt in front of the villagers. Today, one of the majorettes decides to spoil his display.

Sequence 6

Soundscript

Breaking – clattering / banging – rustling – dropping onto hard surface – rustling of cloth – sudden heavy 'froomp' – ripping – heavy object dragging – heavy breathing – breaking – heavy breathing – silence – rustling – silence – 'Looking for something?'

Possible lines of questioning

– Where is this scene taking place?
– Who makes the noise from the beginning almost until the end? Is there only one, or more than one person involved?
– Can you identify each of the sounds? What is causing them?
– Who speaks the words at the end? How is he related to the person or persons from the earlier part of the sequence?
– What happens next?

Suggestions for oral work

In pairs, try to work out exactly what happens in the sequence (go into detail about how big things are, what they are made of, etc.). Then change partners. Try to find out your new partner's version of the story by asking him questions to which he can reply only *yes* or *no*. Once again, try to discover as much detail as you can.

Suggestions for writing

– Form groups of four. Imagine that you are preparing the script for a scene in a TV adventure film. Write out the group's interpretation of the sequence in the form of a script. (A script contains a description of the *set* – that is, the scene where everything takes place – *directions* to the actors, and *dialogue* between the actors.)
– Imagine that the person or persons in the first part of the

sequence could not go to this place himself (themselves) and that instructions must be given to another person to go instead. Write out the instructions explaining to that person what he would have to do.

Vocabulary

See Sequence 2, page 13 for *cut, tear, slash* and *rip*.

- After doing hard work, such as lifting something very heavy, a person would usually be *out of breath*, he would also be *breathing heavily*. If he was a fat man, he might also be *puffing* and *blowing*. After running fast or over a long distance, runners are often *panting*. This is also the noise that dogs make when they are thirsty – with the mouth open and the breath coming in quick gasps.

- Which of these things would *not* make a *rattling* noise?
  a closed door which the wind is moving
  coins being shaken in the pockets
  an old car going over a rough road
  teacups being put carelessly on a tray

  Would the word *clatter(ing)* better describe one of them?

Possible interpretations

- A burglar is looking for something of value in a house he thinks is deserted. He is surprised by the owner.
- A spy is surprised by a security officer just as he discovers the documents he has been looking for.
- A man has been locked out of his own house by his wife. He is sure she has a lover, so he breaks in while she is away. Just as he finds the letters he was looking for, his best friend appears at the door . . .
- A young student who is very forgetful has just got to the airport when he realises he has left his passport in the hostel. He leaves his luggage at the airport and rushes back to the hostel; but on arrival he finds he has left his keys at the airport. He breaks in and searches desperately. Suddenly, a policeman . . .

Sequence 7

Soundscript

High pressure hiss – laughter – loud report.

Possible lines of questioning

– What makes the first sound, or causes it to be made? Is this sound in any way connected with the last sound?
– Who laughs? Why? Is the laughter connected with the first sound?
– Who makes the last sound? What is this sound?
– Where does this short scene take place?

Suggestions for oral work and writing

– Choose a partner and discuss the sequence together. Once you have decided what happens, draw the sequence in a set of not more than five pictures to make up a strip cartoon (use stick figures if you are not good at drawing). When your cartoon is ready, pass it round to the other groups.
– You were writing to a close friend, and had begun to tell him / her in detail about this incident, when you had to break off the letter. You now come back to the letter, but, as you want to catch the post, you keep your description down to the minimum. When you have finished, 'post' your letter to someone in the group.

Vocabulary

– When *gas* or *liquid* escapes under *pressure* it makes a *hissing* sound. In which of the following is the hissing caused by a *leak*?
a jet of water from a hosepipe
steam from a pressure cooker
steam from a central heating radiator
soda from a soda-syphon

steam from the safety-valve of a locomotive
air through the ventilation-hole in an aeroplane

- There are various ways of describing the sudden release of gas
  or liquid: *spurt*, *squirt*, *spray*, *shoot out*, *rush out*, *escape*, *hiss*, etc.
  Which of these words is most closely linked with *sound*?
  Which suggest a smooth, continued motion? Which refer only
  to liquids?

Possible interpretations

- An eight-year-old boy has picked up a soda-syphon at a party
  given by his parents. He has trapped the dog in the corner and
  is happily squirting him. His elder brother creeps up behind
  him and gives him a hard cuff.
- Two teenagers have discovered a fire-extinguisher in the
  corridor of a block of offices. One is 'extinguishing' the other.
  Suddenly the jet of spray hits one of the long neon lights in the
  ceiling . . .
- Young child has discovered how to switch on the gas fire, and
  is about to light it with the aid of a giggling brother / sister.
  Panic-stricken parent arrives just in time to knock the matches
  out of the child's hand.
- Young son is 'testing!' the oxygen cylinders of father's diving
  equipment . . .

Sequence 8

Soundscript

'Early morning' noises: distant clock striking six, birds, train in distance – gradual build-up of traffic, etc. – waking-up sounds – heavy footsteps approaching – rattling / jingling – sudden hard metallic sound.

Possible lines of questioning

- What time of day is it in the sequence? Be as precise as possible.
- How many people are present at the opening of the sequence? How long have they been there? Are they standing, lying, walking, sitting . . .? Where are they? And how did they get there?
- Does anyone else come into the sequence? If so, who is it? At what point does this person enter?
- What feeling (hope, despair, excitement . . . etc.) do the last few sounds in the sequence arouse in the listener(s)?
- If anybody were to speak in this sequence, what might be said?

Suggestions for oral work

Choose a partner. Each of you should be one of the people in this sequence. Decide, with as much precision as possible:
a) how well you know each other, whether your relationship (if there is one) is friendly, formal, one of superiority–inferiority, improving, getting worse etc.
b) how each of you came to be where you are.
c) what each is going to do as from the end of the sequence.
Now work out a short presentation of this sequence using *dialogue* and *monologue*. Give the sequence a conclusion. When you are ready, present your interpretation to another couple; they will then present theirs to you.

Suggestions for writing

Twenty years after this happened, you have become famous. You have been asked to write your autobiography. Describe this incident in not more than 400 words. Mention if any of your feelings have changed after so many years. The 'autobiographies' should then be collected and redistributed. Each person will now read one aloud; the others should comment, suggesting where they think the writer has *lied* or deliberately altered the facts. (In this exercise it is important *not* to put your name to what you write.)

Vocabulary

– Often, when we are tired, bored, worried, in pain, etc. we use sounds rather than words to show how we feel. Here are some of the more common ones:
groan (pain, weariness, disappointment)
yawn (boredom, tiredness)
sigh (boredom, weariness, disappointment)
grunt (surprise, strain)

These words can be used as both nouns and verbs.

– In this sequence, some sounds are distant, others close. And some move nearer or further away. Consider the various ways of describing relative distances:

close	*far-off*	*approaching*	*receding*
near	distant	coming closer	going away
right there	in the distance	drawing near	fading
not far (off)	a long way off	getting nearer	disappearing
	remote		passing

and relative intensity:

softer	louder
stronger	weaker
higher	lower
harder	softer

Possible interpretations

– The night-watchman of an important warehouse (which has been broken into twice in three months) fell asleep at 4 a.m. He was supposed to open the gates at 5 a.m. It is now 5.30.

The owner of the warehouse has had to go home to fetch his own keys. The watchman wakes just as the great steel gate is opened, from outside . . .

- Winter. A tramp managed to hide for the night in a corridor of a large underground station. The guard is coming to open the steel gates before the first train begins to run.
- Last night, a member of an important delegation was arrested in a foreign city for not carrying identity papers. He has spent an uncomfortable night in jail. The conference begins at 8 a.m. and he has had no time to prepare. The guard arrives to unlock the cell door. The delegate is waiting impatiently to be released, but the guard is only bringing breakfast round . . .
- Death Row. The condemned man wakes up; this morning he is particularly sensitive to all the sounds he is hearing for the last time. He hears the guards' footsteps; then the bolt shooting back in the door . . . of the cell next to his.

Sequence 9

Soundscript

'Now let me see. Ah, yes. There.' – click – sigh – chewing – click – 'Ah-ha – click – chewing – click – 'Mm' – click – chewing – click – 'Ooh' – click – chewing – 'Tch! Tch!' – click – chewing . . .

Possible lines of questioning

- How many people are there? Can you tell whether they are indoors or out?
- Is there any special kind of activity going on?
- Can you interpret what the person is feeling when he makes the various noises (ah-ha, mmm, ooh etc.).
- What is the relationship between the people? Do they like each other?
- How long has this scene been going on? What might happen soon?

Suggestions for oral work

Working in groups of three, find an interpretation which satisfies the group. Then decide how this incident might continue. This will involve the characters in speaking. Prepare a short sketch of the incident with words, which will include all three members of the group.

Suggestions for writing

Write a short letter that one of the people in the incident might have written to the other the next day. (This might be a letter of *apology*, of *congratulations*, of *explanation*, of *commiseration*, etc. depending on how you interpreted the incident and who is writing the letter.)

Vocabulary

- *click* is a short, sharp, sudden sound, usually produced by something metallic. It is not usually very loud. Here are some of the things commonly associated with clicking:
  The click of a light switch
           a camera
           a lock being closed
           a TV being turned off
           a handbag being closed

  Click is frequently used figuratively to mean *understand*:
  'He'd been thinking about the problem for hours, when suddenly it clicked' (i.e. the pieces all fell into place).

- *chewing* is just one of the noises people make when they are eating. It is used to describe eating things which are sticky or tough, e.g. gum, toffee, steak, tobacco.

- *munching* is used for food that is hard or brittle, e.g. apples, biscuits, nuts.

- People often use voice noises instead of words to show their feelings. In this sequence, the sounds could mean something like this:
  Ah-ha!   – Now I've got it!
  Mm   – Now, let me see . . . What shall I do next?
  Ooh   – That was unexpected.
  Tch! Tch! – I'm annoyed.

  These sounds do not always mean the same thing. Differences of meaning are usually achieved by changes in loudness or tone.

Possible interpretations

- At the World Chess Championship, the reigning champion is having a very hard match. His opponent is trying to make him even more nervous by remaining completely silent and by persistently chewing gum.
- A photographer is arranging the position of his model for a series of photographs. The model is a mindless, bored person, who never stops chewing gum. The photographer is normally a patient person, but . . .
- A candidate for a very important job in the Foreign Service has reached the final test. This consists of assembling a very

complex model without the instructions. He is being supervised by an impassive retired police officer who is chewing gum because smoking is not allowed. The candidate thinks he has solved the problem, but . . .

- A seaside boarding house: dead silence in the dining-room. An elderly couple (who have already been there for a week) are eating tough meat and passing the salt / pepper / sauce back and forth.

Sequence 10

Soundscript

Rustle – female laughter – male chuckle – female laughter increasing – male giggle – rustle – second female, giggling – buzzer – crescendo of mixed giggling, chortling, sniggering – buzzer – buzzer – hasty rustle – whispers – silence.

Possible lines of questioning

- How many people are involved: how many men and how many women? Where are they? If in a room, what is it like? Small, large, bright, dark, part of a flat, an office? If outside, whereabouts? In a park? On a boat? In the desert? In the jungle? etc.
- Why are they laughing? Is it something one of them has said? At something they are doing, something they are going to do, something someone else has done? Are they worried that someone may hear them? Are they nervous, excited, bored, relaxed?
- Why does nobody speak?
- Why does the laughter stop suddenly at the end?

Suggestions for oral work

The intruder. In groups of three or four, discuss the above questions. Decide who each person is and who the intruder is. Agree upon what is to happen next. Now send your 'intruder' to another group. Each intruder must find out from the group to which he is sent what they were 'up to'. He must also work out who their intruder was.

Suggestions for writing

Imagine that the intruder does *not* in fact enter the room. He or she knows what is going on, and the next day writes a short note to one of the people in that room asking for an apology / explanation / clarification . . .

Vocabulary

– The way people laugh can tell us a great deal about what they are feeling. A laugh may be hesitant, nervous, full-bodied, timid, affected, honest, hypocritical, puzzled, and so on. Consider the following words, and try to imitate the laugh (or the shape of the mouth) that goes with each. What kind of person do you associate with each?

chuckle	titter
giggle	roar
snigger	smile
snicker	grin
guffaw	smirk
chortle	simper

– In this sequence, a *rustling* sound is heard. What kind of sound is *rustling*: dry, muffled, loud, light, faint, deep? Which of the following would not *rustle*?

dry leaves in the wind
cellophane sweet papers (being unwrapped in a cinema)
mice in the attic
sticks in a fire
sheets on a bed
paper money being counted
rain on the window-panes
scent being sprayed
a cat in tall grass

Possible interpretations

– Three students doing Europe 'on the cheap'. They are extremely tired but cannot afford to pay for three hotel beds. One of them then books in and smuggles the other two up to the room via the tradesman's entrance. They are busy settling their sleeping bags on the floor when someone rings at the door.

– A 'surprise' birthday. Father is a crusty sixty-year-old trade union leader who doesn't approve of 'wasting money on luxuries'. His daughter-in-law is determined to show him that life is not all nuts and bolts and screws. She persuades the son and daughter to help transform their father's study into an 'Aladdin's Cave'. They are still decorating at 5 o'clock, but father is not expected back till 6 o'clock. Then the doorbell rings . . .

– Three amateur actors rehearsing the 'bedroom' scene of a farce at the home of one of the girls, whose parents have gone away for the weekend. All three are in bed when the doorbell rings.

Sequence 11

Soundscript

Footsteps on gritty surface – wind whining – distant humming of engine – footsteps – crescendo of engine – hurried footsteps – heavy breathing – engine passes by, extremely close – total silence – wind – metallic chink – footsteps running on grit – same engine returning fast from distance, rising to great roar – cut.

Possible lines of questioning

- Where does this episode take place? Be as specific as possible (e.g. are there any trees, buildings, mountains, nearby?). What time of day is it? What is the weather like?
- How many people do you think are involved? Describe at least one of them. What is he or she wearing? How old is he or she? etc.
- Why is this person here? Where has he or she come from?
- What machine(s) are involved in the sequence?
- What sounds are repeated? Do they alter in any way when they are repeated?
- At one point there is a moment of total silence. What is the reason for this?

Suggestions for oral work and writing

With a partner, listen to the sequence once again. Note down, individually, as much as you can about each sound. Then compare your notes and discuss your differences.

Now, imagine that you are writing the script for a TV film. Write down the directions for this sequence, mentioning where close-ups are needed, where the camera concentrates on a special detail etc. Describe some of the actors' expressions, and add in any dialogue you wish. Your 'script' should not be more than 500 words (though it may cover several pages!).

When you have finished, exchange scripts with another couple. Read theirs, and discuss its weaknesses (and merits) with them. Criticism should be *constructive*!

Vocabulary

- Most interpretations of this sequence will be focused on the idea of *escape*. Consider the following words: *flee, run away, break out*; (to be) *on the run, make a getaway, hide from*; (to be) *chased, hunted, hounded, pursued*. Which of these suggest that the escaper is a criminal?
- In discussing this sequence, words may be needed to describe lonely places, e.g. *heath, moor, desert, wasteland, swamp, marsh, plain* etc.
- When a man is *panting* he may be *tired* or *frightened*, or both. Consider also, *exhausted, worn-out, weary*, and *terrified, panic-stricken, desperate*, etc.

Possible interpretations

- Alaska. Late spring. A lone trapper, who once killed a man in a bar-room brawl, is out inspecting his traps. He hears a small plane approaching (but there is nowhere for planes to land here). He is frightened it may be the brother of the man he killed. He runs; nowhere to hide. The plane passes, extremely close. (We hear the chink of one of his traps as he flattens himself to the ground.) He gets up and runs, but the plane returns, and this time . . .
- Deserted moorland. The kidnapper of a young child is being chased from the air. He is carrying the child over his shoulder. As the plane zooms down on him he takes out his revolver. Then he decides to leave the child and run for it . . .
- Sabotage. Two men have just planted high explosive under the electricity pylons in a lonely part of the country. As they are returning to their car, a small police plane spots them. One of them twists his ankle and falls (we hear his monkey-wrench falling to the ground). His friend does not wait; the sound of the car starting is drowned by the roar of the aeroplane.
- Wartime. A spy, disguised as a shepherd, is trying to escape across the border. In his hand he carries an axe; over his shoulder branches he has cut (to give the impression he was gathering firewood). When the plane appears he at first takes no notice; when it returns, he panics.

Sequence 12

Soundscript

Distant throb of engines – fog-horn (distant) – splashing –
outboard motor approaching – cuts out – oars – engines getting
nearer – sound of grunting – loud splash – excited voices –
engines closing in – confused shouting.

Possible lines of questioning

– Where does this sequence take place? What time of day is it?
  What is the weather like? How many people seem to be
  involved? Fewer than ten? A great number? Only two or
  three?
– Which sound(s) are heard several times in the sequence? Does
  it / do they change in intensity? If so, what does this indicate?
– What state of mind or condition are the people in? Are they
  happy, tired, exhausted, excited, frightened . . .? Does their
  mood change?
– Is any action performed during the sequence? If so, what and
  why?
– Are the people in any danger?

Suggestions for oral work

In groups of three or four discuss the situation. Imagine that you
were all personally involved. Decide how you came to be in this
situation and what action you took. As a result of what
happened here, a court inquiry is held. Each group will be asked
to testify in court. (The procedure is that one group will
cross-examine another, trying to find 'holes' in the group's
story.)

Suggestions for writing

You are a journalist. Send a *telex* message to your paper
describing what happened to *one* of the groups.

Vocabulary

- In discussing this sequence, the names of various types of
  boats will be needed, e.g. (police) *launch, rowing-boat, raft,
  dinghy, fishing-boat, yacht, cruiser, steamer*. What kind of ships
  are equipped with a *fog-horn*? When is this used? What is an
  outboard motor used for? Would you associate it with a small
  boat or a large one?
- What is a *distress signal*? How is it given?
- What kind of goods are usually *smuggled* by boat?
- In foggy weather is the sea usually *rough* or *calm*?

Possible interpretations

- The Mediterranean. A team of amateur divers has been
  working for several days bringing up Greek vases, statues etc.
  from a sunken galley. They have no licence. This is their last
  day of diving; they stay out till sunset. As they turn back for
  shore a high-powered police launch bears down towards them
  through the mist. They cut their motor and row, hoping not
  to be discovered. Too late. One man panics, and throws two
  large vases overboard. The police draw closer and closer . . .
- A light aircraft has crashed in mid-Atlantic. For two days the
  crew and the few passengers have been in open rafts fitted
  with small outboard motors. They have already sent radio
  signals and are expecting help. Now they hear a ship
  approaching. One of the passengers, in his excitement, stands
  up and falls overboard. As the others try to rescue him, the
  boat they are excitedly waiting for bears down on them
  through the mist. But why so fast . . .?
- A fishing territory dispute. A small fishing-boat is deliberately
  infringing the territorial waters of another country. They hear
  a patrol boat approaching, and cut their own engine in order
  to pull in their nets as quietly as possible. Just as they get their
  last net up the side, it slips back with a splash. The patrol boat
  has now trapped them in its searchlight . . .

Sequence 13

Soundscript

Regular thudding – shovelling – grunting – heaving – dragging
then dropping of heavy object – earth being filled in (pebbles
dropping etc.) – car approaching over bumpy road – door opens,
then slams shut.

Possible lines of questioning

- Locate the action (above ground, underground, near water, on
  a building site?). Are there any sounds that indicate how many
  people are involved?
- Is the action at the beginning of the sequence hasty, slow,
  frenetic, leisurely . . .? Is it difficult? Do you think the person
  performing it is alone? If not, who is with him? If so, is he or
  she expecting anyone to arrive?
- Does anyone arrive? If so, who?
- Towards the end of the sequence, a vehicle is heard. How fast
  is it going? What is the road like? Does it stop because the
  driver *meant* to stop there, or because he is interested in the
  action going on?

Suggestions for oral work

Choose a partner. First discuss your reactions to the questions
above and exchange interpretations of the sequence. Now,
decide on *one* interpretation (it may be a new one, or a
combination of your earlier ones if neither of these is
satisfactory). Think of the next five minutes following the end of
this sequence. Some dialogue will take place. Decide who will
speak and write down what they say as if it were part of a play
(even including instructions to the actors). When you have
finished, try presenting your own scene to other pairs.

Suggestions for writing

Read *Public Opinion* by Frank O'Connor (CUP *CELL* short stories). Could you adapt this story to the sound sequence, or, alternatively, could you *write the soundscript* for this story.

Vocabulary

– Two actions will need to be described in this sequence: *digging* and *carrying*.

Here are three pieces of commonly used digging equipment: *spade, pick-axe, shovel*. Which is used for breaking up hard surfaces, loosening rocks, roots, etc.? Which is used for digging a hole? And which for shifting loose earth, sand, gravel, etc? Try to describe the characteristic feature of the shape of each of these.

If an object, e.g. a heavy log, is too big to carry, you may *roll, shove, heave, drag, pull* or *haul* it. These are actions of pushing or pulling rather than carrying.

– Roads in remote districts are usually *untarred* tracks or *dirt* roads. They are generally *bumpy* because of the stones and rocks, and because of the *ridges* and *potholes* caused by the wind and rain.

Possible interpretations

– A travelling salesman, driving through the wilds of North Scotland, runs over a Highland sheep. He knows that few people pass along the road and that the villagers will remember his car. So he decides to bury the dead sheep. In the boot of his car he always carries a pick and shovel, as he often gets bogged down on muddy roads. As he is finishing the hole, the local farmer pulls up in his Land-Rover . . .

– Road workers in a remote country district putting up 'Light no fires' and 'Hunting prohibited' signs. Each signpost is fixed to a ready-made concrete base, which has to be placed 80 cm underground. As they finish their last sign, the pick-up lorry stops to collect them.

– Australia. A remote farm in the West. Ever since his only son left four years ago to work in Adelaide, the father has done all the work on the farm alone. He is now putting in the corner-posts of a new sheep pen. It is 6 a.m. when he sees the car draw up. At the wheel is his son, whom he hasn't heard from since he left.

41

Sequence 14

Soundscript

Receding voices – footsteps – yawn – metal dragging / rolling – yawn – tinkling / sweeping of glass – chink – grunt – metallic tapping – metal dragging / rolling – silence – wind sighing – metal dragging / rolling – pop – scraping – metallic tapping – violent irritation noise – metal dragging / rolling.

Possible lines of questioning

- What has just happened before the sequence begins?
- How many people are involved at the beginning? Later? Who are they?
- Where does it take place? (In a town? A village? A home? A shop? An office?)
- What time of day is it? What is the weather like?
- Who or what is causing the knocking noise?
- Is there any connection between what happens at the beginning and at the end? What will happen next?

Suggestions for oral work

In groups of three, try to work out what really happened. Then turn your story into a sketch where the people speak as well as act. Discuss carefully what they might say to each other in your version of the story, but do not write it down. As soon as you are ready, play your sketch to another group.

Suggestions for writing

- When you have seen another group's sketch, try to write out what they said. Then use your script to act it out for them. They may criticise your interpretation!
- In pairs, try to write a poem of not more than ten lines which gives the atmosphere of the sequence as you understood it.

Vocabulary

- At the beginning, the voices and footsteps *fade away* as they *recede* into the distance. (See also, Sequence 8, page 28).
- The wind is *sighing* in this sequence. We frequently apply other human sounds to the wind (and to other elements). The wind can *whisper, shriek, howl, whistle, moan, roar.* Water, usually in a stream, can *murmur, chatter* (over stones) *lap* or *lick* at the bank.
- There is intermittent *tapping* in this sequence. We can *tap* on a door, window etc. *Tapping* is always done lightly. *Knock* is a more general word, and suggests a heavier action. We can also *bang on* a door; this is an even stronger action. If we *rap* on a door or on a table we do it very hard and expect people to pay attention. The same is true for *hammer*, though often this denotes desperation (she hammered on the door, hoping that someone would hear her). *Drumming* on a table with fingers or on a wooden floor with the heels often suggests impatience.

Possible interpretations

- It is 2 a.m. and the last customers have just left Pierre's bar in the Latin Quarter of Paris. He closes the blinds and sits down for a last glass of wine with his wife before going to bed. Someone knocks on the shutters, but when Pierre opens them, there is no one outside. He closes them again, and again someone knocks. In a rage, he flings them open again, and finds himself face to face with . . .
- It is midnight on Christmas Eve and Jones the butcher has just sold his last turkey and shut up his shop. While he is settling down to a glass of port with his wife, there is a knocking on the shutters. The first time he opens, there is no one. The second time, he is very angry, but finds himself face to face with Father Christmas – pointing a pistol at him . . .
- The boss and the rest of the gang have gone off leaving Charlie and his wife guarding the two prisoners. Each one is in a cell with a roller metal door. Charlie has been told that the two prisoners must not communicate with each other, but just as he is settling down to a drink, one of them starts tapping a message. He goes to the door and threatens the prisoner. As he sits down again, the other one starts tapping . . .

Sequence 15

Soundscript

Babble of voices – gradually coming to a stop – silence – gong.

Possible lines of questioning

- Where are all these people?
- Why are they all talking at once? Are they all talking about the same thing?
- Why does the talking gradually come to a stop? Have the people noticed something? What could it be?
- What is the meaning of the last sound? Does it announce the beginning of something? If so, what could it be?

Suggestions for oral work

Each person should spend a few minutes thinking about his own interpretation of the incident. Then, as a class, discuss your interpretations. Try to collect as many *different* versions as possible. One person can act as secretary, so that no ideas are lost.

Suggestions for writing

- One of the people present at this occasion keeps a diary in which he/she records impressions of what happens in his/her life. Write out the entry for this event. (You will probably need to make reference to the kind of people who were there, the atmosphere, and what they were waiting for.) When you have finished, exchange your diary with a friend, and read what he/she wrote.
- In threes, write out the script for a radio commentary on this occasion. The radio audience can hear all the noises in the sequence. It is your job to tell them what you can see.

Vocabulary

- The noise made by a large group of people all talking at once can be variously described:
  the *hum* of conversation (when it is relatively low and unexcited)
  a *hubbub* or a *babble* (when it is confused and quite loud)
  gabbling (when it is very rapid and confused)
- Several verbs can be used to describe the gradual reduction in the level of conversational noise:

subside	die / quieten down
peter out	calm down

Note that all of these words refer to a reduction in noise at a given place, whereas *fade away* usually refers to a noise which lessens because it moves farther away.

When the noise is *increasing*, these words can be used to describe it:
swell / build up to a peak / climax / roar etc.

Possible interpretations

- A group of foreign tourists has gone to visit a Buddhist temple. Their excitement dies down when a monk appears. He strikes the gong to announce the beginning of the ceremony.
- Some celebrities (film stars, etc.) have been invited by a millionaire to a very 'special' party at his luxury villa. They stop talking when they see the millionaire coming down some steps towards them, wearing a bull's head mask and nothing else. He strikes the gong and . . .
- Outside Newgate prison in the eighteenth century. An excited group is waiting to see a famous highwayman hanged. The talking stops when the hangman appears and strikes a gong to announce that . . .

Sequence 16

Soundscript

Underground train approaching station – slowing down – hiss of opening doors – feet receding down tunnel – doors close – train moves off, sound recedes – footsteps – locking of concertina gates – silence – echoing footsteps running – shaking / rattling of gate – scream.

Possible lines of questioning

– Is there any sound that might indicate what time of day it is?
– Does this sequence take place in an open or a closed space? Do you think this space is brightly lit, gloomy, absolutely dark . . .?
– The opening sounds suggest something moving. What is moving? In which direction? How fast? Why does it stop?
– Towards the end of the sequence, footsteps are heard. Whose are they? Where does that person come from; where is he or she going?
– Is there any sound that strikes you as being unreal, out of place, mysterious, or for any reason hard to explain?

Suggestions for oral work

Discuss the above questions with the class as a whole. Note down some of the interpretations offered. Now divide into groups of three. Each group will attempt to solve the 'mystery' in its own way. When they have reached a satisfactory explanation they should invite another group to find out their answer by questioning. Questions should be worded so as to produce three possible answers: yes, no, not quite.

Suggestions for writing

The police are attempting to reconstruct the events of this day. Write down in note form an hour-by-hour description of this man's activities during the day.

Vocabulary

- If doors make a *hissing* noise when they shut, what kind of doors are they? Are they sliding doors, or doors which open inwards or outwards? How do they close? With a *handle*, a *catch*, a *lock*.

   If a gate *rattles* when it is closed, what is it probably made of? Is it solid or can you see through it?

- Other words likely to be needed if the sequence is thought to take place in an underground railway:
   platform
   guard
   entrance / exit
   compartment / carriage
   corridor

Possible interpretations

- A.D. 2009. The world is divided into three great cities, one above ground, one on the sea and in the air, and one underground. The inhabitants of the underground city do all the hardest jobs, and come up above the ground only to work the machines of the two 'superior cities'. At night they are taken back by underground trains. This night, a worker decides to try and escape along one of the long corridors. But when he gets to the end of the corridor he finds it is barred by a metal grille – which is electrified.

- A former spy (now retired and living in a quiet country cottage) dreams of an incident that happened to him thirty years ago in a certain European capital. He had been trying to shake off two men who were 'tailing' him. By constantly changing trains, he succeeded in losing one of them. When he got off the last train of the night, he tried to cut up the 'Entry' corridor, only to find it blocked by a metal gate. When he turned round, the other man was already on him . . . He was found the next day, half dead, his arms tied behind him to the metal gate. Now he wakes up; his arms are twisted through the metal bars of his old-fashioned bedstead . . .

Sequence 17

Soundscript

Cicadas – sigh – winding followed by ticking – clinking – liquid pouring – music – tapping – rustling / scratching – scrunching – sigh – tapping – 'Jim' – cicadas.

Possible lines of questioning

- What time of day is it?
- Which country is it happening in?
- Is it happening inside or outside?
- How many people are involved? Who are they?
- What is the word the woman says at the end? What does it mean?
- How do you explain the tapping noise? Is the woman expecting it?

Suggestions for oral work

In groups of four, work out an interpretation of the sequence. Decide also how the action continues (who does what next? what is the result?).

One person from each group should now move to the next group. He is to take the role of a journalist trying to find out from the group what happened. The group members answer his questions as if they had witnessed the event. The journalist can ask for clarification or justification as often as he likes. He should *take notes*.

Suggestions for writing

- The 'journalists' return to their original groups. Each group then writes up in the form of a short article the story which the 'journalist' has collected. The articles should be taken back to the group on whose story the article is based. They can then make any criticisms of mistakes, omissions, etc. which they notice.

- Alternatively, groups write out a brief scenario of a film. This sequence was the opening scene of the film. What happens in the rest of the film?

Vocabulary

- The best word to describe the insect noises which go on throughout is probably *trilling*. A *trill* is always a high-pitched, continuous sound made up of very rapidly repeated single sounds, e.g. if you run a ruler quickly along the teeth of a metal comb, you produce a trill. *Trilling* is most often associated with birds, however (see Sequence 4, page 19).
- For *sighing* and other human noises, see Sequence 4, page 20.
- For *clinking*, see Sequence 2, page 13.

Possible interpretations

- The (South American) plantation owner has gone on a business trip to the next town and will not be back until tomorrow. His wife is alone. It is midnight. She is waiting for her lover, Jim. Meantime, she writes a letter of farewell to her husband and screws it up as she is not satisfied. When she hears the tapping she goes to open for Jim, but it is not Jim. It is . . .
- A rich young widow is on holiday in the Mediterranean. She has hired a villa, and spends each evening alone with her memories. When she hears the tapping, she thinks it is her guard dog, Jim, trying to get in. But when she goes to open the door, she finds the handsome young fisherman she met earlier in the day.
- A young couple have bought some land on a tropical island and have just finished building their dream home. The local people were very much against the couple's settling here. The husband, Jim, has gone to see the village headman about some damage they have caused. She thinks it is him tapping at the door, but when she opens she finds . . .

Sequence 18

Soundscript

Heavy object crashing through foliage – sound of metal being unclipped – heavy thud – foliage – human noises – disoriented footsteps – distant barking – Whoosh! (from distance) – barking closer – rifle shot – (cut to echo chamber) 'O.K.?' – 'Mmm, not bad but . . .'

Note: Try playing this sequence, but stopping just before the people speak. Go through the exercises at this point. Then play the *whole* sequence, including the speaking. What difference does this make to the interpretations?

Possible lines of questioning

– What is the first sound in the sequence? Does it suggest upward or downward movement? Is the body that is moving (or being moved) heavy or light? Where does it come from?
– Where does the action take place? Can the people involved see what they are doing? What do they feel – fear, excitement, despair, hope, relief. . .? What are they doing? How are they moving – walking, crawling, sliding, running . . .?
– Why do the dogs bark? Whose dogs are they?
– Who are the people speaking at the end of the sequence? Were they involved in the action? What will be said after: 'Mmm, not bad, but . . .'?

Suggestions for oral work

Listen again to the recording, this time with a partner. Imagine that this is only *part* of an incident. Together work out a *beginning* and an *end* to the sequence. Make sure that you have a plausible explanation for all the sounds. Now join up with another pair and exchange interpretations.

Suggestions for writing

This incident happened, directly or indirectly, to you. You have been approached by a newspaper to write an article for them on what happened, and what you think of it. (You may, if you wish, use the interpretation of another group.) Write down the *notes* from which you plan to write your article, making clear which points you intend to stress.

Vocabulary

– It is likely that discussion of this sequence will come round at some stage to the setting of the action. Some of the following words may be needed:
bush
jungle
(dense) undergrowth
forest
wood
branches / creepers

– The sound that comes between the barking noises towards the end will be open to various interpretations. In order to avoid influencing these interpretations, it is advisable to let the students explain in their own words what they think they have heard. They might then be reminded of the following:
fireworks
Very lights
flares
SOS signals
orientation flares

– The last words 'Mmm, not bad, but . . .' are unfinished. Whatever the interpretation may be, this sentence is likely to be resolved with constructions such as the following:
it would have been better if . . .
you / they / it should've (been) . . .
I'd prefer . . .
couldn't you . . .
it wasn't long / short / loud / high enough
it didn't . . .

Possible interpretations

– An Army training course. The Commander-in-Chief is

51

watching videotapes of operations in which cadets were parachuted into 'enemy' territory (heavily forested), and had to find their way to 'safety' without being caught. The officer in charge of the operation wants to know what the Commander thinks of the videotape, but the Commander is interested only in the military value of the exercise.

– The owner of a large country house has decided to hold a *son et lumière* (festival with fireworks) in his park in order to raise money for repairs. He has called in a professional to arrange the spectacle. For special effects, men have been placed at different points around the park to set off the big coloured rockets, etc. The owner is watching a preview of the spectacle together with the organiser . . .

– A film studio. The director is looking at the first rushes of a war film set in Borneo. He is not satisfied with the quality of the colour, but does not want to say so openly.

Sequence 19

Soundscript

Confused voices – clattering – knocking – noise goes on – louder knocking – noise subsides – silence – puffing – cough – 'Ladies and Gentlemen . . .' – rapping – silence – rapping + 'Hey!' – water – 'Coming, dear!'

Possible lines of questioning

– Is this happening in one place or more than one? Where?
– Who is the man who says 'Ladies and Gentlemen . . .'? Why is he there?
– Is he connected with the man who says 'Hey'? If so, how?
– Who is the person who says 'Coming, dear'?
– What do you expect to happen next?

Suggestions for oral work

In pairs, work out an agreed explanation of what happened and what will happen next.

Each pair now joins another pair to form groups of four. The group exchanges its two versions, and must then agree on one of them as the more convincing.

The groups of four now join each other to form groups of eight. Once again, the two versions are discussed and the better one is chosen. Finally, the remaining versions are discussed by the whole class.

Suggestions for writing

– Write a letter to a close friend (someone else in the class) describing the incident as you saw it. The letter should be given to the person in the class to whom it is addressed.
– In groups of four, write a *stop-press* news item of four lines to cover this incident. (The *stop-press* column in a newspaper includes items which came in too late to be included as proper

articles. It therefore has a style resembling that of a telegram.)

Vocabulary

- For the noises made by *conversation*, etc., see Sequence 2, pages 13–14.
- For the *clatter* of crockery see Sequence 6, page 24, and for the *clinking* of glasses, see Sequence 2, page 13.
- For the *subsiding* of conversation, see Sequence 15, page 45.
- For *knocking, tapping, rapping*, see Sequence 14, page 43. The sound made in the second part of the sequence (followed by 'Hey!') would be described as *rapping*: it is hard and impatient.
- Before starting, the speaker *cleared his throat* with a nervous cough.

Possible interpretations

- A young politician is making his first public speech at a banquet for his party members. As he begins to speak, his mind goes back to a little earlier in the evening when he was trying to make his wife get ready in time.
- A 'punk' star has been awarded a prize by his home town. The mayor has organised a banquet, but half-way through the meal the star has still not appeared. The mayor decides to play for time by giving a long starting speech. Meanwhile, the star's manager is frantically trying to sober him up and get him out of his bath.
- A well-known industrialist has just risen to speak at the National Federation's annual dinner. Unknown to him, one of his rivals plans to discredit him by staging a scandalous scene at the dinner, using a notorious person. The dinner is now in its last stages, and unless he can get the notorious person out of the bath he will not be able to create the scandal he had planned.

Sequence 20

Soundscript

Cries – snapping, rustling – shouting – steps in water – water – barking – shot – silence – low whimper – silence.

Possible lines of questioning

- What is the first sound you hear?
- Is the incident happening inside or outside? What kind of a place is it?
- How many people are involved?
- How many types of animal are there?
- Is all the action happening in the same place?
- What is the explanation of the sudden loud noise towards the end of the sequence?
- What kind of an event is going on?

Suggestions for oral work

In groups of four, try to work out a convincing explanation of the incident. Before starting, take an English dictionary and open it at *any* page. Look at the *fifth* word defined on the page and write it down. Close the dictionary and open it at random again. This time, write down the *seventh* word defined. Now see if these two words suggest any ideas for finding an explanation for this sequence.

When all the groups have finished, discuss the exercise as a class. How useful were the words you found in the dictionary?

Suggestions for writing

Form groups of *eight*. Decide on *one* version of the sequence. Now, each member of the group should write down on a slip of paper one sentence which relates to the incident. The sentence should not be longer than ten words, and no one should show his sentence to anyone else. The sentence written can be simply descriptive, or it can relate to the feelings of someone in the incident, or to the feelings of the writer. The slips should be collected and given to another group. Each group at this stage should have eight sentences which it has received from another group. The group now looks at the eight sentences it has received and arranges them in the best order possible so as to form a poem about the incident.

Vocabulary

- Dogs make a variety of noises. In this sequence there are hounds (hunting dogs) which are *baying* or *yelping* at the beginning of the sequence.
- When someone is completely *soaked* in water, he is *drenched*, *Wet through, wringing wet*. Here there is a sound of water, squeezing out of clothes, then of someone *wringing* them dry, accompanied by the *splashing / dripping* of water as it hits the ground.

Possible interpretations

- A long-distance runner has challenged the Master of the local Hunt to a race in which he will be hunted by a pack of hounds. A poacher prowling in the wood shoots the man, thinking he is an animal.
- A group of children have just finished school and go off through the woods to a nearby pond. While they are floating their boats in the water they hear a shot. They find a man who has had a hunting accident. His dog is whining next to him.
- A thief has just broken into a country house. On his way out he has been discovered and is now being chased through the woods by men and dogs. He plunges into a river, swims across and there finds one of the dogs facing him. He shoots, but not to kill it . . .

Sequence 21

Soundscript

Wild Hungarian music – glasses on tables – smashing of glasses – shouting / drunken laughter – loud double hand-clap – silence – footsteps across broken glass – female voice 'Uh huh? Uh huh. O.K.' – footsteps back over glass – revelry starts up again.

Possible lines of questioning

– What *kind* of music opens the sequence? Is it music you often hear in your country? Is it sad, gay, old-fashioned, experimental . . .? Where would you expect to hear it?
– Who is listening to the music? Is anyone *listening*?
– What is going on at the same time as the music? Has it been going on for a long time?
– Why does the music suddenly stop? What does this tell us about the person whose footsteps we hear?
– When the woman speaks, does she sound offended, pleased, interested, bored . . . or is it not possible to tell from her tone what she is thinking?
– Why does the music start up again?

Suggestions for oral work and writing

– Choose a partner. Exchange your reactions to the questions above. Then decide what exactly is said to the woman. At the most, it should be two sentences. Write your two sentences clearly on a slip of paper. After five minutes all slips of paper should be collected and redistributed. Each pair will now have a new sentence. They should take it in turns to read their sentence(s) out aloud to the whole group. Everyone will now try to guess the interpretation of the sequence from this sentence. (The pair which wrote the sentence will, of course, not take part until several suggestions have been heard.)
– This incident happened to you (or you were present).

Although you do not keep a regular diary, you have made a fairly thorough record of what happened on that occasion. Write out the relevant extract. Do not forget to mention what happened *later*. It is important that your writing should be *anonymous*, so that it can be circulated for others in the group to read.

Vocabulary

– Discussion of this sequence is likely to centre on the idea of *festivity*. English is peculiarly deficient in single words to convey the idea of 'having a great time'. *Merrymaking* is too prim to suit more than the most innocent festivities. Here are a few expressions that might be more suitable:
living it up
having a ball
painting the town red
let oneself go / enjoy oneself
have a party / celebrate
go wild / mad

– We do not know what the lady is *asked* in this sequence, but we can tell from her reply that she *agrees* to do it. Depending, of course, on the degree of politeness and insistence, the request might have opened in any of these ways:
Will you . . . / would you . . . / can you . . . / could you . . .?
I'd like you to . . .
D'you think you could . . .?
What I want you to do is . . .
All I want you to do is . . .
Couldn't you (just) . . .
I'd be very grateful if . . .
If you don't mind, I'd like you to . . .
I wonder if you would care to . . .?

Possible interpretations

– A middle-aged couple from Hull decide to cycle their way through central Europe. Their journey has attracted some interest in the press, and by the time they reach Hungary they are well-known. One Saturday they cycle into a village where a wedding is in full swing. They are invited to be guests of honour. The festivities have already been going on for fifteen hours when the sequence begins. The host, weary, drunk, but still standing comes over to ask Mrs Baldwin if she would sing an English song in honour of the newlyweds. Mrs Baldwin is 'game for anything' . . .

– Members of a British trade delegation to Bratislava are being entertained by their Czechoslovak hosts. Several of the more virile members are already asleep on or under the tables. The young interpreter, however (who has been drinking with the best of them), is still fresh. It is at this point that the head of the Czechoslovak delegation decides it might be wise to get the speeches over. Would she mind interpreting?

– A (low-budget) film is being made on the life and times of Liszt. The producer, preferring the exotic to the authentic, packs as much passion as he can into each scene. The leading actress is now fed up with the whole film, but cannot back out as she is under contract. In this café sequence she is supposed to be dancing wildly with the young Liszt on a table. Neither actor is happy with the idea. The producer now realises this and comes over to suggest that they dance on the floor. The actress agrees, without any great enthusiasm.

Appendix 1 Words used to describe sound in English

The purpose of this appendix is to indicate the precision of language that *could be* aimed at, once the students have become familiar with sound. It is not expected that students will acquire the vocabulary given in this section, and the teacher should not feel that he is obliged to teach these words. In group discussion, one would not often expect to hear, for instance 'I heard the grating of a metal grille' or 'there was a light tinkling in the background . . .' etc. After a sequence has been worked through, however, the teacher may like to select certain sounds for detailed consideration. These lists will provide a useful point of reference.

The words set out below have been grouped on an 'ad hoc' basis in terms of the way they are produced or by what produces them. Wherever possible a commonly associated word or collocation is given in brackets after the word, e.g. *squelch* (mud). This list is not intended to be exhaustive, however, and should be used in conjunction with a good dictionary.* A dictionary will give additional information regarding parts of speech (though in fact most of the *verbs* used here are unchanged when used as *nouns*) and the more usual connotations of the words.

1 Sounds made by humans
By the mouth
in eating/drinking

chew	lick (lips)
chomp	smack (lips, chops)
crunch (bones, toast)	guzzle (beer)
munch (apples, biscuits)	splutter
suck (sweets)	gulp (milk, tea)
slurp (tea, coffee)	

after eating/drinking

belch	gasp (for breath)
burp	grunt (of satisfaction)
hiccough	sigh

* See, for instance: Roget's *Thesaurus*; *Oxford Advanced Learner's Dictionary of Current English* by A. S. Hornby; *Longman Dictionary of Contemporary English*.

associated with illness

cough	spit
sneeze	spew
gargle	croak
retch/puke/vomit	sniff/snuffle
wheeze (chest)	clear (the) throat
hawk	chatter (teeth – with cold)

to show amusement

laugh	simper
snort	howl (with laughter)
guffaw	roar (with laughter)
bellow (with laughter)	shriek (with laughter)
giggle	yell
chuckle/chortle	cackle
titter	squeal (with delight)
snigger/snicker	

(*note also*: a ripple, wave, surge, of laughter)

to show anger/displeasure

shout/bawl/bellow	growl
yell	grind/gnash (teeth with rage)
roar	grumble
shriek	mutter
screech	snarl
howl	scream

to show pain

scream/howl/roar (with pain)	gasp
groan	grunt
moan	cry/sob
whimper	squeal/yell (with pain)
whine	yelp
wail	shriek

ways of articulating

whisper	jabber
murmur	gabble
mutter	slur (one's speech)
mumble	lisp
stammer/stutter	chant
chatter	drone (on and on)
twitter	pipe (up; in a piping voice)

(*note*: and most words from the previous three sections)

ways of making musical or rhythmic sounds

sing	warble

chant
hum
whistle
yodel

coo
croon
trill

miscellaneous
yawn (with boredom/fatigue)
sigh (with disappointment/resignation)
grunt (with satisfaction/irritation)

*noises with meaning/exclamations (a full range of these is not
   possible without a recording to demonstrate their use)*
ooh! aah! (how lovely!)
ah! (what a relief)
oh? (really? indeed!)
tch! (what a nuisance!)
tch! tch! (shocking!)
ouch/ow! (it hurts)
phew/whew! (that's a relief,
   that was hard work)

hey! (what are you doing?)
cor! (great)
whoops! (that was a near thing!)
pooh/pah! (I don't think much
   of that)
ooof! (what an effort!)
mm/uh-huh (I'm still listening)

adjectives commonly used to describe voice quality
(*note*: verbs can also become adjectives ending in -ing; these are
not included)
wheedling
whiny
hoarse/croaky
husky
gravelly
rough/raucous
harsh/coarse
grating/rasping
gruff
throaty
thick
deep/low
strangled
muffled
hollow
muted
mellow/warm
rich
melodious
gentle/sweet
sexy

piercing
penetrating
strident/shrill
sharp/high
staccato
resonant/resounding
booming
thin/piping
droning
cold/cool/icy
bluff
breezy
oily
honeyed
smarmy
polished (tone, accent)
steely
plangent (tone)
la-dee-dah (affected)
high-pitched
low-pitched

velvety
dusky
wavering/quavering
shaky

treble
soprano/alto
tenor/baritone/bass

By the nose
sniff/sniffle

snivel

sneeze

snort

snore

snigger

By the stomach, intestines, etc.
rumble

gurgle

grumble

fart

By the feet
shuffle/scuffle

tap (toe, heel)

stamp/stomp

scrape (boots)

plod/pace

drag (heels, feet)

march (in step)

clump (heavy boots)

patter

thud (landing on feet)

pad (barefoot)

slither (on something slippery)

tip-toe

swish (through bushes, or on

paddle (through water)

   skis)

squelch (through mud)

creak (sound of leather)

By the hands
clap ⎫
slap ⎬ (face)
smack ⎭

snap ⎫
tap ⎬ (fingers)
drum ⎭

whack (bottom, shoulders)

beat/pound ⎫
hammer/batter ⎭ (fists)

clout (head, neck)

crack (knuckles)

rasp (rough palms rubbing

scratch (with nails)

   together)

rap (with knuckles)

stroke

rub

pat

By the bones/joints
crack
snap
creak

2 Noises made by animals
Birds
in general
warble

chirrup

squawk

chirp

pipe

trill

hoot

twitter

cheep

screech

caw

cry

wings

flutter

flap

whirr

beat

swish

in particular

hoot ⎤

shriek ⎬ (owl)

screech ⎦

caw ⎤
⎬ (crow, raven)
croak ⎦

coo (dove)

cry ⎤

squawk ⎬ (gull)

screech ⎦

quack, cackle (duck)

honk (wild geese)

cluck (hen)

cheep (chick)

crow (cock)

chatter (magpie, starling,
 parrot)

Dogs

bark

whimper

wail

yelp

sniff

growl

bay (hounds)

whine

howl

yap

snarl

Cats

mew

hiss

purr

spit

Horses

neigh

snort

wheeze

whinny

munch (oats)

swish (of tail)

stamp ⎤

drum ⎥ (of

clatter ⎥ hooves)

thunder ⎦

Pigs

grunt

snuffle

snort

squeal

Cows, etc.

moo

low (cattle)

bellow

bleat (sheep)

Snakes

hiss	spit
rustle	slither (through grass)
rattle	

Elephant, rhino, etc.

trumpet (elephant)	bellow (buffalo)
snort	stamp

Lion, wolf, etc.

roar
growl $\Big\}$ (lion, tiger)   howl (wolf, hyena, jackal)

Monkeys, etc.

chatter	screech
bark (baboon)	

Insects

buzz	drone
whizz	chirp
whirr	trill
hum	whine (mosquito)
tap, flap (against window, light, wall)	flutter

Rodents (rats, etc.)

gnaw (through wood)	scratch
scurry	scramble
patter (mice)	rustle (in grass)

3   Sounds made by water/liquids

trickle	drip
drop	patter (raindrops)
splatter (mud)	lap (small waves)
wash (sea on the shore)	gush (geyser, hose)
rush	churn (by propeller)
slop (from bucket)	bubble
beat (rain, hail)	boom (surf, waterfall)
	whistle (steam)

4   Sounds made by the wind

whistle	thresh (branches)
whine	howl (storm)
roar (storm)	moan
rustle (leaves)	whisper (breeze)
wail	sigh (breeze)

65

5 Sounds made by metal

click	chink (coins)
tick	clang
clash	rattle
scrape	ring
clang	tinkle
jingle (coins, bells)	jangle ⎫
clink (glass, coins)	clank ⎬ (chains)
rasp	grind
grate	

6 Sounds made by wood

thud	chafe (against hard surface)
creak (boards)	clatter (wooden shoes)

7 Sounds made by cloth

rip	tear
rustle (clothing)	flap (sails, clothes on washing-
swish (skirts)	line)
rumple	flutter (flag)
split (tight clothes)	rend

8 Sounds made by breaking

crash	smash
crack	snap
splinter	split
shatter	crunch
explode	twang (tight string)
ping (tight string)	burst

9 Sounds made by striking (percussion)

knock	tap
rap	bang
clang	clap
chink	clink
clank	slap
smack	flick
jingle	jangle
clump (boots on floor)	hammer
thud	drum
slam	clatter
batter	ring
thump	boom
judder	beat

10 Sounds made by rubbing/friction

creak	rustle
rattle	squeak
scratch	shuffle (cards, feet)
grate	rasp
swish	grind (teeth, gears)
slither	drill, bore (hole)
scrape	slide

11 Sounds made by explosion (release of pressure)

pop (cork)	fizz
hiss (gas)	bang
burst	boom
thunder	whoosh, whizz (of rocket, fire-
gush (water)	work)
roar	crack ⎫
detonate	report ⎬ (rifle)
echo	spurt (blood)

12 Sounds made by cutting

snip (scissors)	rip (cloth)
tear	chop (axe)
saw	slice
scythe (grass)	whine (electric saw)

13 Sounds made by falling

thud	flop (into bed)
plop (into water)	clatter (to the floor)
drip	tumble
slither (down slope)	slide
crash	patter (raindrops)
clonk (metal)	bump
slump (body)	plummet
thwack	

14 Sounds made by cooking

splash	bubble
hiss	fizz
sizzle	simmer
splatter	crackle
pop	spit
hiss	

15 Sounds made by fire

crackle
hiss (wet wood)
whoosh (of flame)

roar (of flames)
fizzle (when put out or dying
  out)

16 Sounds made by engines, machines, etc.

whirr
hum
tick (tick over)
chug (slowly)
grind
squeak
ring
bleep
rev (car engine)
thump (steam-hammer)
spin

purr
throb
pound (heavy motors, mills)
clank
creak
rumble
buzz
judder (heavy machinery)
choke
churn
wail (siren, alarm)

17 Sounds made by musical instruments

strum (guitar)
blare ⎫
blast ⎭ (trumpet, radio)
twang (strings)
oompah (brass band)
pound (piano keys)
and
to make a racket/din

drum
tinkle (bell, piano)
pluck (strings)
ping
scrape (bad violinist)

18 Miscellaneous sounds

(re-) echo
crumble
boom

resound
rumble

Appendix 2 Examples of written material to which reference can be made when doing the 'writing' exercises

1 Poems with a strong focus on *sound* and movement
2 An extract from a film-script
3 Extracts from diaries, a notebook and a telegram
4 Headlines

1 Poems

The end of school

Bell rings, boys run, doors slam,
distant feet in the playground;
only the silent steps of the cleaners.

Colin Chapman, age 12

(From English Project, Stage One, *Family and school*)

Seasons

Spring: Slippy, drippy, nippy.
Summer: Showery, flowery, bowery.
Autumn: Hoppy, croppy, poppy.
Winter: Wheezy, sneezy, breezy.

Sydney Smith

(From English Project, Stage One, *I took my mind a walk*)

Squishy words
(to be said when wet)

SQUIFF
SQUIDGE
SQUAMOUS
SQUINNY
SQUELCH

69

SQUASH
SQUEEDGE
SQUIRT
SQUAB

Alistair Reid

TRIS-TRAS
is scissors cutting paper

KINCLUNK
is a car going over a manhole cover

CROOMB
is what pigeons murmur to themselves

PHLOOPH
is sitting suddenly on a cushion

NYO-NYO
is speaking with your mouth full

PALOOP
is the tap dripping in the bath

Alistair Reid

(From *Ounce, Duce, Trice* by Alistair Reid)

House moving

Look! A house is being moved!
    Hoist!
    Jack!
    Line!
    Truck!

    Shout!
    Yell!
    Stop!
    Stuck!

    Cable!
    Kick!
    Jerk!
    Bump!

Lift!
Slide!
Crash!
Dump!

This crew could learn simplicity from turtles.

Patricia Hubbell

(From *Catch Me a Wind* by Patricia Hubbell)

2   Extract from a film-script
(for reference in *writing* exercises involving film-scripts)

VARIOUS VOICES [*off*]: H'ya, Buck!. . . Howdy, Buck!. . . How's
    things in Bisbee, Buck? Have a good trip?
[*Meanwhile, the* Shotgun Guard, *who has guarded the treasure box
from Bisbee, jumps down to the sidewalk.*]
SHOTGUN GUARD: So long, Buck.
[*Men begin unhitching the horses.* Buck *acknowledges the cheery
greetings as the* Wells Fargo Agent *in Tonto pushes his way through
the crowd.*]
WELLS FARGO AGENT: Howdy, Buck. Got that payroll for the
    mining company?
[Buck *kicks the box which is under his seat.*]
BUCK: She's right here in this box.
[*The* Wells Fargo Agent *climbs up to the top of the coach, calling to a
colleague as he does so.*]
WELLS FARGO AGENT: Give us a hand with this box, Jim.
BUCK: Jim, I'll pay you that $2.50 when I get through.
JIM: Okay.
[*The two agents get the box down and carry it off between them –* Buck
looks over his shoulder to the other side of the coach.]
BUCK: Now you kids get away from them wheels!
[*He starts to get down and calls to the men who are leading the horses
away.*]

(From *Stagecoach*, a film by John Ford and Dudley Nichols)

3   Extracts from diaries, a notebook, and a telegram
a) *Mon.* 7
    Lost wallet at Paddington Stn. Ticket inside, of course.
    Phoned Geoff – wasn't in. Tried buying ticket by cheque –
    wouldn't accept it without Banker's Card. Started crying. . .

ev'one staring at me . . . got angrier and angrier, began yelling at ticket-clerk. Clerk called police! Ended up being charged with breach of peace . . . While charging me they searched ev'thing I had. Found wallet in lining of coat . . .

b) FEBRUARY 7 – *Monday*

08.00 – See President (Chairman? check) ELCAM.

10.00 – Check arrival time flight SAA 7549
Book taxi for 13.00. Get Davies to draw £50!!

12.00 – *Long distance* call ex-Bogota. Check table booking.

13.00 – Lunch + 2 people (?). Phone 47352 before 14.15.

15.00 – Yoga man may call – warn Davies.
PTT – phone still unconnected. Why?
Photocopies – collect.

c) *Feb. 7, 22.15*
Gatecrashers cut lights. Three injured in dark. Nothing reported missing. Complaint – police took 25 mins to arrive. Descriptions of g-crashers don't tally: owner of estate says one fat, 5 ft 2 ins, and two over 6 ft. Wife – one was a woman in disguise! Request *no* publicity. Refused further questions.

d) YOUR CABLE AWAITED EX LONDON STOP NON RECEIVED STOP ORDER CANCELLED UNLESS IMMEDIATE REPLY RECEIVED STOP CONTACT BREWER 235768 PRE MIDDAY STOP HITCHIN

4 Headlines

ESCAPED TIGER RECAPTURED

KILLER AT LARGE NO MORE!!

TERROR PICNIC ON HAMPSTEAD HEATH

RARE BENGALI TIGER STILL AT BAY

RSPCA PROTESTS AT TIGER SHOOTING

TIGER IN THE TEACUPS

Bibliography

Byrne, Donn and Wright, Andrew, *What Do You Think?*, Books 1–2 (Longman 1975)

Grellet, Maley, Samuel, Soulie *et al.*, *Slide into talk* (Hachette 1978)

Hodgson, John, *Uses of Drama* (Methuen Educational 1978)

Jupp, T. and Milne, J., *Talk English* (Heinemann 1971)

Maley, A. and Duff, A., *Sounds Interesting* (CUP 1975)
  Drama Techniques in Language Learning (CUP 1978)
  The Mind's Eye (CUP forthcoming)
  Variations on a Theme (CUP 1978)

Also of interest: BBC Enterprises publish a series of sound effects on disc.

35